First Verse

A collection of poetry by Luke A. Chase

Title: First Verse
Subtitle: A Collection of Poetry by Luke A. Chase
Author: Luke A. Chase
Publisher: Whippoorwill Press, a division of
                  Whippoorwill, LLC
                  Overland Park, KS
                  913-341-7104

ISBN 0-9741968-0-0   Library of Congress Control Number 2003106762

Cover and book design by Ron Daniel, Firefly Marketing Communications, Kansas City, MO and initial concept by Dan Starkey, Starkey Marketing, Minneapolis, MN

Printed in the United States of America
by Signature Book Printing Inc., Gaithersburg, MD

This book was printed on acid free paper.

FIRST EDITION

Table of Contents

Introduction   vii
Light   13
    Musings   14
    Appetite   15
    Beware   16
    Noses   17
    Soap   18
    Inspiration 19
Life   20
    Hollyhocks 21
    Learned   23
    park swings 24
    Sight   25
    Marble Shooters 26
    Gift   29
    Savor   30
    Peace   31
    'lection time 32
    Night Song 33
    Wonders   35
    My Tree   37
    Legacy   38
People   39
    To Bonnie 40
    Fifteen   41
    Of All My Teens 42
    Carmen   43
    This is for Owen 47
    Dear Ed   49
    Mindrift   50
Observe   51
    Infinitum 52
    Breeding   53
    9 11 01   55
    Youthsong 57
    My Mind/Random 58
    Yield   60
    Moonsail   61

Table of Contents

Memorium	63
Opine	64
Wee Dram	65
We're Ordinary Folk	
Acclaim	
Faces	70
Oh, Poo!	71
Celebrity	72
Call Me L.	73
Want	74
Mirthy!	75
Sufferage	76
Opus	77
Selfless	78
Laws	80
On Leaden Feet	82
Love	83
A Ringing	84
Kisses	85
Affection	86
What Measure	87
The Fall	88
Rare Kisses	89
A Taste	91
Love Bug	92
Journey	93
Love's Plight	94
To Wed	95
Our Time	97
She's Here	98
The Suitor	99
My Hate	100
Remember	101
For Joan	102

Table of Contents

Lord   103
    More   104
    Forgive   107
    Knowledge   108
    Prayer   110
    Stars   112
    Spark   113
    My Stars   115
    Miracle   117
    Praise   118
    Drink Deep   121
    Flight   123
    Surprise   124
Afterword   125
    Steve Chase   126
    David Chase   128
    Kirt Chase   130
Tributes   132
    His Mark's On Me   133
    Abbott!   136
    All The Bad Things...   140

INTRODUCTION

Introduction

Reflecting along the path of one's life feels like a strange thing to do. Not that we all don't do it, but sometimes we realize that some of the twists and turns would have made our lives different. Maybe not for better or worse, but just...different. You know: "...if my parent's lives had gone in another direction, then my life could have been ..." But I guess we all do that kind of thing. We think about those times in our lives in which we were given choices, and we have a what-if moment, wondering if the chosen fork in the road would have played out another way if we'd chosen the other one.

I've often wondered what may have happened to me if I hadn't come across Luke Abbott Chase in my earlier wanderings, trying to find myself. As the Vietnam war was winding down, I had just come out of the Army with a disappointing experience. I was trying to find the what-do-I-do-next chapter in my life, and I happened to apply at the Columbia Daily Tribune where Luke was Advertising Manager. I'll never know what he saw in me that day. Maybe it was nothing. More than likely he just needed a live body. But I look at that as a seminal moment for me: having Luke Chase as a boss for the succeeding 4 or 5 years has made a profound difference in the way I think about the world today, and about how I lead my life even now.

They say that most people never get to work with a mentor. I can believe it. Luke was a mentor, a father-figure, a friend and ally, and someone I looked up to then as well as now.

It was a magical time at the 'Bune, as we all comically referred to our place of employment. It was a great time, and lifelong friends were created. I should say that the kinds of bonding relationships among our little peer group at the 'Bune has never happened again in my life, and I don't expect it will ever happen again. And, in the discussion and development of this book with a few of those old friends, it's become pretty obvious that we all felt the same way. We still feel the same way. We joked around, but we worked hard. We had disagreements, but we all had what amounted to the same problems, so nothing was ever too big to resolve. Life by committee. The 'Bune became a microcosm of our extended lives, and Luke was always there to make it better.

Luke wasn't so much of a boss as he was a leader. He knew when to insist and when to let things play out. He knew how to teach, even if he didn't know he was actually doing it.

This was the mid-70s, and the 'Love' generation was giving way to the 'Me' generation, but I stayed comfortably rooted in the past; in my rock 'n roll days as a musician. I remember desperately trying to get back into the music business in some way. I was hanging out with musicians and trying to be cool. I was playing clubs some weekends, and trying to book other bands into them too.

One day at the 'Bune, I happened to mention something about the "real" people to Luke. I was referring to the Alan Ginzberg and Hunter Thompson types that grew both rich and famous by bucking the societal norms and writing about it. I really thought the alternative point of view was a big deal. At that time, the campus of the University of Missouri was rife with long haired, pot-smoking, anti-war people and half of them were the instructors. And they were the ones I respected; the Real People. Luke just laughed at me. "Real people, you say?" Without saying it, this is what he meant: "...who the hell is a 'real people?' They're all real people, asshole! Rich or poor, intelligent or dumb as a rock, agnostic or kiss-your-ass Catholic. It don't matter." A life's lesson, well learned. Thanks, Luke.

After Luke's retirement from the newspaper business, he began to follow his own dream; a lifelong love of poetry. I'm sure he's written hundreds of verses - many more than what is contained in this volume. But as we've renewed our old friendship as adults, he began to send them to me periodically, as his thoughts and feelings translated into verse. In the beginning, I was simply flattered that he was willing to share his private thoughts with me. After all, we'd not really talked in years. But we fell into a normal rhythm, as though the length of time had not really passed at all.

When both my parents died in 2002, Luke sent me a poem he had written that I thought expressed exactly the way I felt about life. I used it in my mother's funeral, and many commented on how beautiful it really was. Luke was flattered to have been 'published,' and that's what gave us all the idea to create this book.

I want to go on talking about my memories and fondness for Luke Chase. But it's not my book. It's his. And I can think of no better way to honor a man we love than to help him realize his own dreams.

Dan Starkey
March, 2003

LIGHT

MUSINGS

He lives a world away, you know,
some secret place inside my brain,
just now and then he comes to me,
and sings a song with new refrain.

From galaxy to galaxy,
he soars throughout the universe,
and with his pen celestial,
he writes in stars for me a verse.

To all who claim these lines aren't mine,
and to their origin divine,*
the truth I share with only one,
he's inspiration's friend; and mine!

*find out or foretell by inspiration;
by magic; or by guessing; predict.*

APPETITE

Her lunch to fix a spider must,
to trap her prey her web intrust.
The spider's style be not impugned,
for so by nature was she tuned.

For each our hungers, feed we must,
and spider-like our instincts trust,
to spin a web of new delights,
and so endear our appetites.

A menu of exotic fare,
concocted recipes so rare,
a whispered promise in the dark,
alike set fire to nature's spark.

Man's hunger, then, was named by fate,
but appetite his hunger sate.
His wants and needs
decide the matter.
But more of former
and less the latter.

BEWARE

Beware that rainbow in her hair,
that turns the sun her way to stare,

nor list' the lute her sweet voice plays,
and spurn her lips: Her kiss betrays:

But if you can't deny her touch,
her ling'ring spell you fear so much,

then to her bed your plot arrange,
for now her diaper needs a change.

16

NOSES

What shame: It mars your beauty so!
That thing enjoys such prominence:
Your countenance it so obscures, ~
seems fixed there 'twas by Providence.
Just suppose that nature gave us
a warning signal in our pants,
a pale green cloud softly glowing,
that would betray our flatulance.

But 'tis not so that mark you bear;
yours stands alone for all to see,
No cloud could possibly disguise
its own universality.

From fam'ly tree there oft times falls,
strange fruit whose heritage not be;
of hair of red and freckles, too,
give doubt to parents' certainty.

Pale clouds of green nor hair of red,
Can quite compare to that unique
eruption grown between your eyes,
like something add to your physique.
And of that thing should dare we speak?
Your nose? For cry'n out loud, your nose!
By any other name, a nose!
That protoplasmic growth! Your nose!

SOAP

Oh, how I treasure
that exquisite pleasure
of renewing my innermost hope
in anticipation
of participation
in a bath with a new bar of soap.

That miserable sliver
once generous giver
of suds luxuriously held sway
lies dead in its dish
not knowing my wish
now just to throw the damned thing away.

INSPIRATION

———————————

These days I wonder at the time
I spend in search of fleeting rhyme.

While crafting lines I'm not averse
none but with myself converse.

In days of youth as one suspects
my thoughts were naught but beer and sex.

Inspired thought my brain's infusing
but beer and sex are less confusing.

LIFE

HOLLYHOCKS

Behind Aunt Amy's house they grew,
two rows of blooming hollyhocks,
astride a path their colors flew,
like butterflies in brand new frocks.

The path itself, a grassy spot,
was bordered, too, with whitewashed rocks,
that shone by moonlight like as not,
as daylight shone by hollyhocks.

At pathway's end, a private place,
just room for one, or two at most,
oft times its privacy embrace,
when nature's call demands a host.

My Uncle Stanley built the thing,
choice one by twelve and two by four,
nailed straight and true by plum bob string,
with strong iron hinges at the door.

Through many a season's change it saw,
and many a tipsy Halloween,
from winter's freeze to springtime thaw,
survived, but worn, those years between.

Inside the place, for darkened nose,
stray shafts of sunlight shot through chinks,
where lazy mists of motes arose,
as if in search of milder stinks.

How strange it is through life we bear,
the brunt of time's old worn out tricks,
the commonplace of yesteryear,
today's replaced by stone and bricks.

Her house, that place, are long gone now,
it's asphalt paved for blocks and blocks,
a victim of the progress plow,
but nary of blooming hollyhocks.

LEARNED

By now you've heard the world is round,
but with both feet upon the ground,
and now you've learned where love is at,
then what's it matter, round or flat?

A common bean seed in the groun',
grows roots and sprouts, knows up fromdown,
our top paid guys, for all they know,
could learn some more, jus' watch beans grow.

And why through life we meditate,
on some philosophy so great,
it leaves unsolved what nature knows,
who gives us life and why it grows.

park swings
swing with kids
swinging

and teeters totter
tots teetering

little boys
on stilts
walk stiff legged
in the air

cold skies
heavy with gray
give way
to blue brightness
springing

great green earth not now frostbitten
yawns and stretches

while robins
scratch for worms

it must be time
for me to wake

SIGHT

What thrill the sight from mountain crest,
of ice and cold and snow possessed!
Sound the deep of great seas swelling!
Ken the crash of tall trees felling!

Weigh the gold in a young girl's hair;
sun-freckled nose, tanned shoulders bare.
Chicken frying, tomatoes red.
A puppy sleeping by my bed.

How saw I these with one sense stole?
Listen! Other senses enroll,
my sight becomes a vision whole.
Touch! Feel! And the eyes in my soul.

MARBLE SHOOTERS
an exposition

On ground ground bare by boys' bare feet,
'neath ancient arched Piss-Elum tree,   (1)
as on a challenged plain they meet,
their fight late formed from chivalry.

On stick-scratched earth a circle's drawn,
to mark the contest's boundary,
it's there they meet, their weapons drawn,
their fav'rite assures victory.

Bright colored marbles are the game,
each globe at risk inside the ring,
who wins the most wins most the fame,
with skill, some luck to it they bring.

Some spheres of smaller size are known,
as Pee-Wee; and their less colored kin,
are chips into the gamble thrown,
and shooters now their game begin.

From drawstring bag of leather stored,
his cache of marbles he has kept.
most cherished one of all his hoard,
the one for gold he'd not accept.-

His taw! His taw! His aggie taw,   (2)
of stone, deep amber swirled with light,
reflections of moon chips strike awe   (3)
in eyes of boys upon first sight.

'Knucks down!' 's the cry to all who play,
'No fudgin, neither!' 's a steadfast law.
Bare knuckles, earth chapped, flat must lay.
No inchin' up to move your taw.

And now the taw line must be set,
its distance from the ring surveyed,
so none to small advantage let,
before the game be ever played.

Now comes the lag, a kindred skill,
from ring to taw line taws are cast,
those marbles landing closest 'twill,
decide the shooters first to last.

At last the contest will begin,
'for keeps' the name this game they play,
best shooters then more marbles win,
and losers play another day.

To grip his taw demands some skill,
his thumb he locks inside his fist,
his taw held 'gainst his finger still,
by knuckled thumb its pow'r resist.

These digital gymnastics hone;
let fly from fist his thumb strikes taw,
to ringward as a missile thrown,
'mongst spheres as from some giant's paw!

See amber aggie taw set out,
sent crashing, shooting marbles through
the ring a' scattered all about,
as if a whole platoon he slew.

You shoot until you miss 's th' rule,
and should your taw be trapped inside,
it's then at risk another's jew'l,
some lucky shooter's shot decide.

And that's the game that ages knew,
as played by boys six thousand years.
'Twas marbles in Tut's Tomb they threw,
the same as found near Grecian biers.

But now the game's become extinct,
a victim of what's civilized,
seen now in lighted tube's precinct,
as skill and dare today's not prized.

*(1) Piss Elum: Idiom, local perhaps, refers to
common Elm Tree.
(2) Taw is the shooter's marble. An aggie taw
is fashioned from agate.
(3) An agate taw, after use, becomes chipped, and the
chipped places left on the surface reflect light in the shape
of a minute half moon.*

GIFT

———

You fret one moment's mindless heat,
and vow its storm you'll not repeat,
but when that vow is still unkept,
thin sorrow's tears I'll not accept.

It's true your youthful passions own,
your love's dispense as on loan,
to lesser purpose I have known.

So now this plan to you propose,
it's one more true than you'd suppose,
wrap up your love in one box fit,
and give to me the whole of it.

SAVOR

A friend of mine retires at nine,
and rises again at seven.
His hours between are well defined.
His life's a loaf that's unleavened.

In his life's book he's a saver,
of pennies and pounds without halt.
Yet in his life there's no savor.
For in his life's loaf there's no salt.

So now when he writes his last score,
and tallies his days on earth o'er,
his sum's a column of cipher.
He'll start life anew as before.

PEACE

Take heed the work the hangman does;
his work that's best falls down his door.
His noose aside he hurries home,
and with his kids plays on the floor.

To mount a task and see it through,
What peace! What peace of mind enhance,
without regard for good or ill,
nor give a single backward glance.

Not mine that peace of mind! for mine's
forever in darker season,
and naught will know the where or why
God alone and I the reason.

'LECTION TIME

There's lots to say 'bout apple pie,
'bout babies kissed and motherhood and sin,
hot August days, spring chickens fry,
long sweaty nights and voters drinkin' gin.

It's best you meet him face to face,
your neighbor, friend, turned statesman for a spell,
in shirt and tie he takes his place,
on stumps the county 'round, his speeches swell.

'it'sa wrasslin' match in hoarse toned shouts,
with holds none barred and falls to count so few,
a contest run to late night bouts,
another match the next night will renew.

This season's work decides the choice,
of candidates November's ticket show,
Republicans will have no voice,
our chosen statesmen we already know.

And this is how our system's run
big city frills and fancy talk decline,
our home grown style's excelled by none,
in Little Dixie here it works just fine!

NIGHT SONG

―――――――

Here comes the night!
Cold dread that visits me,
In the space behind my eyes,
shows me scenes I hate to see.

Black deeds long forgot,
From darkness dragged to light,
cavort and dance unclothed,
and undenied within my sight.

This punishment I endure,
Life sentence I nightly pay,
The pain eased, Oh so briefly,
with the coming of each day.

WONDERS

When first I saw Mount Fuji,
a wintry course we lay,
shippin' out from Leyte Gulf,
north to Yokohama Bay.

A cloudy-rainy, blust' ring sky
makes the sea turn gray.
To see that snow peak in the mist
can take your breath away.

It's a wonder to me now,
of all the places I have been,
my memory flashes back to me,
to another bygone scene.

I see myself a sunburned boy
that I'm remembering,
my belly to the ground,
sippin' water from a spring.

The Gateway to the City,
I say it's truly so,
that stately span at sunset,
takes on a Golden glow.

I saw the ancient Buddha,
and I swear he winked at me.
And I've sunned the beach at Monaco
by a blue seductive sea.

Now my memory rushes back to me,
a laughing, splashing din,
of swimmin' in a creek,
wearing nothing but my skin.

Today what's real is virtual,
a half-world felt and seen,
limited and bound around
by an infernal lighted screen.

If I could, I would bring back,
the youth of yesterday,
when the wonders of the world,
were a short, bike's-ride away.

MY TREE

Say, have you seen my wondrous tree?
It started out a little sprout
outside my door where I might see
it grow and grow with branches stout.

It captures cool 'neath leafy shade,
from heat and glare of summer sun,
and leafless stands in winter made
to leaf again from buds begun.

And so have passed my seasons, too,
from leaps in spring to falls in fall,
my tree it seems to see me through
those disappointments dared recall.

I yearn for heartfelt recompense,
for fruit to feed my peace of mind,
for seed for my new life commence,
for balm my bandaged soul to bind.

One moment's rest, of solitude,
beside it breathes a cure on me,
a warming inward rectitude
My Wonderful Contentment Tree

LEGACY

All that that is of beauty grown,
Soft sounding chords in harmony,
That beat to nature's symphony...
Caress their hearts all creatures known!

Just feel new cells of life blooming,
In swelling waves of births given,
Unite in single song risen,
To all earth's ends echoes looming.

What marvel this orchestral song,
So sung as when the world began,
And passed down generation's span,
To all the human race belong.

And of those voices one was mine,
My song was strong but short in time,
In verses sweet, I thought sublime,
And now pass on to sons of mine.

PEOPLE

TO BONNIE LASS
Female Scottish Terrier

Hail to thee, wee princess!
I kneel before thy throne,
and honor thee thine lineage,
Yea, wishing 'twere my own,

I served two Princes before thee,
born of thy stubborn clan,
fearless, faithful and true
to the family of man.

All they meals I serve thee.
and at they bath attend thee,
and at thy pleasure, hold the door,
lest some indignity offend thee.

When I meet Peter at the Gate,
but one regret I've got.
I've not another life to live,
to serve just one more Scot.

FIFTEEN

A mystic number is fifteen,
not man, nor boy, but in between,

As on a threshold, entering,
to all the hurts that manhood brings,

Yet looking back to early years,
so marked with bruises, cuts and tears,

Rejoice today, forget the pain,
you'll never be fifteen again.

For Alex

OF ALL MY TEENS

Of all my teens this is the end.
It's not forever youth will spend.

So gimme a break to primp and preen.
When May is here I'm just nineteen.

My future's die is not yet cast.
Let me discover life's a blast.

There's time enough to find my queen.
When May is here I'm just nineteen.

For Matthew   5 3 01

CARMEN

When called upon to write this piece,
my first response was... No!
For who would dare disturb my peace?
My pearls on swine bestow?

And then I'm told this tome must be,
about some ancient broad,
that with my pen must shamelessly,
commit poetic fraud!

So then I sought some sucker share,
some blame in this affair.
My muse! My muse! He's got a flair,
with words I wouldn't dare!

"Hey, boss. You need a classic line,"
he says to me my Muse,
"I got this phrase I thought was fine,
my pal of old to use."

"'She walks in beauty, like the night.'
Now there's a line that clicks!"
May be, I said, but not so right,
for vertically challenged chicks!

Besides, you swiped that line from George.
That really took some brass.
Alive today his name you'd forge,
with his good foot kick your.......

"'My love is like a red, red rose.'
Now there's a line that's used.
By any other name a nose....
Boss, you got me confused!"

Don't fret, my Muse. Just take a break.
Old Bobby Burns won't mind.
With larceny I'll make my stake,
in Hallmark cards I find.

But now I vow from tricks refrain,
I hear she's got some smarts.
Who needs a babe what's got a brain?
Well, all the Woods, for starts.

For high eye-cues and talents, too,
the Woods are full of that.
All products of genetic stew,
from Mom and Dad begat.

Besides her own, she celebrates,
the birthdays of her brood,
son Jerry's was the first of dates,
then all the rest debuted.

Another son, she called him Phil,
and then a girl or two,
of these young Caryl topped the bill,
and Cathi followed through.

With young'uns in and out the door,
and all those mouths to feed,
both Mom and Dad together swore,
to fill their soul felt need.

To live and share a loving place,
the joys, and yes, the tears,
now even time cannot erase,
though Dad's been passed these years.

Now looking back when she was young,
a long, long time ago,
before her madding youth was flung,
she longed for Christ to know.

The church at Wilkes and Seventh Street,
she spent her early years,
her off'ring lay at Jesus" feet,
and never in arrears.

To grease her path to heaven's joy,
and have some heavenly fun,
no need a man o' th' cloth employ,
her daughter married one.

And now at last perfection reach,
theology out the ears,
herself a swingin' sermon preach,
no doubt it's He who cheers.

It's plain to see she comes on strong,
with God and all the Saints,
who else would let her live so long,
and with so few complaints!

Happy Birthday, Carmen

Luke Chase et al

THIS IS FOR OWEN

You promised me that you'd come back,
take me home with you some day.
But that was a long, long time ago,
we lost touch somehow
somewhere along the way.

Shoulda called you long before now,
'cause we need some preparation...
where we'd meet, what time we'd leave,
I've last minute calls to make
'fore my final separation.

On second thought, we'd best hurry.
For I must leave here right away.
You pick the time, the place, I don't care
Just let me know
and I'll be there.

DEAR ED

I've found the place ye oughter be,
away from traffic's snarls,
at parkside sippin' on yer tea,
an' watchin' passin' girls.

'sa pastime fit fer a gentleman,
an' 'ighly cultured, too,
with friendly nods more often than,
ya'd see at London Zoo!

It's 'ere ye'll spy a warmin' smile,
from nannies pushin' prams,
their flirtin's in the best of style,
with just a peek at gams.

The park, the girls, the smiles are true
so, pray not be misled,
this place is far too good for you,
I'll take your place instead!

MINDRIFT

You'd pity her her bleak abode,
where madness and cold darkness hide,
inside the circles of her mind,
that marks, the place where hope has died.

From sun to sun she courts an ache,
lain deep within her body's core,
the cause of it she's long forgot,
some deeper hurt her heart had bore.

'Twa' then she set her mind adrift,
upon a calm unbounded sea,
that is for her a state of peace,
a quiet, endless reverie.

1 27 01
Dedicated to Katie Baumgartner

OBSERVE

INFINITUM

A silken haze of indigo,
caresses hills of stately pines,
while springtime sun its warmth aglow,
again new span of life defines.

Beneath the snow in patches left,
green stirring cells await their birth,
in heated beds that nature's cleft,
close by the heart of Mother Earth.

Though pestilence and famine bring,
to mankind horrors through the years,
comes war our sons its hateful sting,
leaves broken bodies bathed in tears.

While men their faith in wars and kings,
their lives relied on walls and towers,
cannot by means these petty things,
hold back the spring nor blooms from flowers.

BREEDING

That pride in antecedents kept,
in family bible pages leapt,
to heights of bloodlines blue to be,
set hope on breeding quality.

What works for livestock and their kind,
known traits of parents' well defined,
not so with human dam and sire,
their offspring's born from night's desire.

Now clad in ill fit elegance,
thus won in cosmic game of chance,
files claim to birth of higher fashion,
in truth he's child of baser passion.

Ask not you then of reasons why,
offshoots of family tree belie,
their lineage of ages try,
account for kids dropped from the sky.

9 1 1 O1

My eyes despise those things I see,
Those fearful shrieks, "It cannot be!"
Grotesque catastrophe! Look there!
Unreasoned hate ignites the air!

Of hurt, unmeasured pain we bear,
Beneath a mountain of despair,
Entombed in instant death, conspired
By chance and sons of Hell inspired.

But why, Oh why this deadly stroke,
Their message sent through fire and smoke,
Why not commune in tones benign?
The God they love's the same as mine.

9/28/01

YOUTHSONG

Come sing your song to me and pray,
your days of youth with you will stay.

Forever young so be your song,
an anthem sung through ages long,

Its lyric and melodic line,
thrive on while lesser tunes decline.

But then your crafty songster's skill
grows dull, and now your voice is still.

Through all the songfests you have led,
your song lives on but youth is dead.

MY MIND/RANDOM

Must I defer to molecules
That science says control my life?
That sure as hell genetics rules
and some sore enzyme chose my wife?

When I was young I'd not allow
some silly thought disturb my brain.
All fun and smiles I'd disavow,
from drink and dance always refrain.

My goal was to my mind enhance,
to build it, shape it to my will,
with no respect for luck or chance.
Success was mine to claim until ----

I long to play with older boys
with light and sound and noise
a world where high priced shrinks abound
and Cadillacs my toys.

My offspring were computer raised
and to their tubes devout
while growing up the most they feared
was power going out.

When art defends its own offense
and fails in just the trying
it breathes alone for recompense
while beauty's slowly dying.

My mind's become my sepulcher,
as sure with stone and mortar made,
where naught of mercy dare confer,
where shreds of love lay, left decayed.

YIELD

In season, petals gently fall,
And voices far, low softly call,

To gather up the harvest yield,
From crops laid by in nature's field.

My season's crop will soon be grown,
As my bloom's petals, ere long blown.

MOONSAIL

Thank God for men whose hearts obeyed
their faith in future days that they'd
entertain some silly notion
in sailing ships cross the ocean.

Come clear your mind of limits lest
you'd think 'twould be some kiddies' quest
from two and two are four start out
to split an atom's all about.

For ages now earth bound were we
from local orbit not set free
but now commune with moon and stars
and someday soon sail up to Mars.

MEMORIUM

A murmur from the mountain peak,
descends across the snow locked plain,
these cold kept, windswept prairies speak,
still blemished not by human stain.

"It's Peace!" they cry. "Sweet Peace has died!
and nevermore her life renew.
We seek a tomb her spirit hide.
No ordinary grave will do!"

WEE DRAM

Yer journey begins
on a broad barren plain,
Disappointment your guide,
through tears shed in vain.

So, don't waste yer breath
askin' reasons like 'why?'
The day ye were born
ye were startin' to die.

Now take a wee dram
and drink to yer past,
and count yer next heartbeat,
it may be yer last.

They'll gather yer kin
to a kirk in the glen,
and celebrate sadly
with singin' of hymns.

Yer days on this earth
their brevity cry,
the day ye were born
ye started to die.

WE'RE ORDINARY FOLK

We're ordinary folk
and we eschew
the ostentatious. We lean toward,
rather painfully toward
the gracious.
Invited to a formal ball,
white tie, tails and all,
bejeweled tiaras optional,
my sweet spouse
feels above reproach
wearing her simple Tiffany
diamond brooch.
For we're ordinary folk,
plain ordinary folk,
just ordinary folk are we.

Our friends drive Bentleys, ~
Porsches
and Rolls Royces
But when we pick a motor car
our unanimous choice is
the unobtrusive,
four door Jag-u-ar,
done out in racing green,
one for her and one for me,
for we're ordinary folk you see,
plain ordinary folk are we.

There is a set
that goes yachting,
all around the globe
a'trotting.
Ours is a modest little vessel.
Accommodations for ten we keep,
plus three more,
for the cook, first mate
and steward
also need a place to sleep.
We're ordinary folk,
plain ordinary folk are we.

For dwelling places
mansions in the Hamptons
are too spacious,
and Benedict Canyon's
not our speed.
Palm Springs is passe now,
now that Frank's... um
passe now.
That place we can't abide.
The mountainside
is where we reside.
We prefer our
little place in Vail,
the one in Aspen, too.

And our little shack
in the Exumas
is where we like to hide.
For we're ordinary folk,
just ordinary folk are we.

We have an invitation
to a White House State Dinner,
and for a weekend
with Barbra at Malibu.
At the risk of a social breach
with the Commander in Chief,
or to suffer,
Streisand's thunder,
we've opted to jet
down under
and meet new found friends
at Bondi Beach.
For we're ordinary folk,
plain ordinary folk,
just ordinary folk are we.

ACCLAIM

Come beat the drum, the prince announce.
Adorn his way with cheering throng.
Beneath his lovely visage counts
the hearts of those to him belong.

But that's the census of today.
Tomorrow's prince may soon arise,
replace the prince of yesterday,
and claims his own the public's prize.

Your name's not cut on some stone pile?
No songs composed to celebrate,
the heights you stormed with such great style?
A pity your fame bloomed so late!

Then build a paper manse to house
ungoverned hordes, a twisted race
whose knotted proverbs now espouse
pathetic dreams in this poor place.

FACES

Give up your dogged, breathless pace,
your futile maddening quest,
forever searching for the other face,
his sins yet unconfessed.
Deceipt's the common coin you found,
common decency the other.
Your looking glass alarum sound!
You need look no further.

OH, POO!

Oh, poo! on scribes who glorify
the blooming rose and butterfly.

Why not a bat or wallowed hog?
or even worthless yaller dog!

While beauty with beholders lie,
who says we must see eye to eye?

Those rose-eyed poets don't know squat!
Just look for beauty where it's not!

CELEBRITY

Before you go, write down your name,
thus in my book record your fame,
that I to all the world may show,
so future generations know.

This passing moment not deny,
for soon your presence we can't buy,
and though that time should be unkind,
yet to your memory we bind

What! Your name's writ' in golden script!
That it may shine beyond your crypt?
What foolishness for you to show,
that yours 'mong other names should glow.

But then your name was always small,
your reputation it was all,
and when its luster may be lost,
then from my book your name be crossed.

CALL ME L.

Dear Lord,
deliver me from fancy folks
whose first names
I'll never see.

Is the thing so horrible?
It engenders thoughts deplorable
And makes you think it's better
to replace it with a letter
followed by a period, of course.

Forget for giving up the given name,
in this awkward situation.
But heaven forbid we forgo
the friggin' fervid punctuation.

by L. Abbott Chase

Let's lower the bar to cordiality.
It would be swell
if you would call me
by my first name, L.

WANT

What craves your heart so dear, my son?
For laurels earned in battles won?

For precious stones on rings of gold?
For gems and things of wealth untold?

Or do you seek the crowd's applause?
Or praises raised for vaunted cause?

Can care you give your name's renown?
It's heavy rests the victor's crown.

Then weigh you well those things you need;
for you may pay for all your greed.

MIRTHY!

I know a man
who has a plan,
to keep alive
the myth of mirth.
He's searched for mirth
o'er all the earth,
even the north of
Firth of Forth.

          Firth of Forth?

"Howdy," he greets
to all who smile.
Saudis he meets,
their smiles deviled.
A dearth of mirth's
upon the earth
ev'n among the
peerage of Perth.

          Peerage of Perth?

He finds reverse
to be perverse,
and sees at last
his ride's a hearse.
Wrapped up, his shroud
he's chaffing in,
days end,
dying of laughing
in.

          dying of laughing?

SUFFERAGE

Consider here my candidate,
his platform is to stir up hate.

"Stand you not close to me," his vow,
"For I'm holier than thou."

He translates God's word on order,
loves his mother as he oughter,
and on Sundays walks on water.

Yes, I know it's SUFFRAGE. This is different.

Let's take a poll and see
just who the winner might be.
We can save a trip that way
and stay home on Election Day.

OPUS

I read your last piece
and I must submit
you wasted your time
toiling over it.

If 'twas intention
to flout convention
then
'twas a-big success.

Words cannot mention
my deep contention
that your invention
was hatched
from your
intellect annulled.

My analysis
is your cerebral
paralysis
led extenuating
circumstance create,
a craftily
conventionless,
artfully
inventionless
opus that's
pedestrianly
dimensionless.

SELFLESS

—————

From birth you learned your garb to shine,
with smiles, some tears and glinting eyes;
Sweet dulcet tones and kiss combine,
to coin a currency of lies.

With these your moral debts you paid,
without respect for others' needs;
You got the best of bargains made,
the feast on which your ego feeds.

Your glowing garment came alive,
and everything it was was you;
Your true self then dared not survive;
It died along with all that's true.

Come see your self,
it's hanging... there;
You'd hardly know it,
it's so bare.

That scar you see,
there love once dwelt,
that tear the place,
tenderness felt.

All this you thought,
composed your soul,
you lost as part,
of heaven's toll.

To lose your self's
a worthless fine;
Come 'long with me;
I'll show you mine.

LAWS

Men in blue marching row on row,
fearless leaders in a valiant fight,
girded by laws of government's might,
teach youngsters just to say no.

A Catechism! Sermon without point,
must to the choir oft repeat.
The congregation's 'cross the street,
in a circle, passin' 'round a joint.

With TV screens their cause enhancing,
it's religions' right to be spoken
of all of God's Commandments broken,
even those that lead to dancing.

Church and State so long divided,
in this fray united they stand,
by force of law and God's own hand,
the lives of thousands now decided.

Evil's a sickness of the frail,
addiction's a crime and must be paid
in sentences by the judge assayed
the cure: throw his ass in jail.

That sentence by half and half again.
could make old Hippocrates cringe,
like taking a hit from a used syringe,
could bring on a malady of equal pain.

See your name on a court docket?
Know the likeness of the law;
smoke it, buy or sell it, detect a flaw?
You're busted!
if you got it in your pocket.

***

Humorists tell lawyer jokes
to uproarious applause.
Ha! Ha! Ha! The joke's on us, folks.
One reason we got so many lawyers
is we got so many laws!

Our nation's rooted in the law.
On that we can agree.
But do we really need a law
that protects myself from me?

ON LEADEN FEET

On leaden feet they trudge toward,
Horizons lit by hopes forlorn,
And shameless seek in one accord,
Ambition's mantle, threadbare worn

Not less but more their goals get set,
For prizes gilt but not of gold,
At gath'rings of their peers are met,
To share in one conceit enrolled.

A monument to nothingness,
Raised aimless up by spotlights press,
It beckons those whose minds possess,
A worth not nil but less and less.

LOVE

A RINGING

A little bell inside of me,
stands watch, and rings when things go well.
I notice when you're close to me,
it rings out loud! A great big bell!

I pray you have a bell like mine,
that sounds alarm when I come near.
Then hand in hand, our bells align,
and make a sound we both can hear.

KISSES

———

What is that sound I hear, a sigh?
It's how your youth remembers it,
a warming moment on her lips,
or when her kiss bids you goodbye,

Hot moonwhite nights 'neath circ'ling stars,
a drink of fragrance deeply flood,
from blooming honey locust trees,
your heart's locked up by love's sweet bars.

Kisses, like your days, are measured.
You should not waste a single one.
Invest each kiss with care today,
tomorrow will each be treasured.

AFFECTION

---

affection hides in divers spots...
in apple pie and biscuits browned...
it's sometimes poured from coffee pots...
in layered cakes with frosting crowned...
in chicken fried, its gravy made...
in deaf ear turned to nightly snores...
in calming tones for tempers frayed...
and patience lent for put off chores...
in...

WHAT MEASURE

What measure dare I make of thirst?
My glass, you see, is filled.
Good fortune's friend has marked me first,
his wine before me spilled.

When I address my dinner plate,
what's absent from my fare?
Its preparation's never late,
My larder's never bare.

Ecstatic heights are commonplace
at home, the place I live.
My neighbors thrive on peace and grace,
and all my faults forgive.

My life's complete, or so it seems,
I need not want for much.
My wants are filled to all extremes,
I need a tender touch.

THE FALL

In storybooks in love we're said to fall,
as from a cliff or down an icy slope,
into a pit or hopeless swirling flood.

If so then why employ a word so small,
to designate this state with which to cope,
whose length and breadth we've never understood.

The depth of love old poets have explored,
and given measure to its ecstasy,
in search for words and images befit.

For lovers true the fall's to be deplored,
for having loved the truth they clearly see,
when love is all, the fall's not half of it.

RARE KISSES

No need to hide behind your eyes,
your secret's safe with me,
nor clad your heart in false disguise,
your thoughts I plainly see.

And so to me your love confess,
how worn a lie can be!
To other loves your love profess,
the same's your love for me?

Perhaps it's your capacity,
affection's larder store,
and then dispense judiciously,
to one or two or more!

If that be so, then I'll expect,
my share, no less, no more,
and value of your kiss respect,
far less than 'twas before!

A TASTE

The taste of jealousy we crave,
Its venom sweet our souls enslave,
And through life's long addiction bear,
Pure torture born of dark despair.
Because rare beauty's only lent,
And charm's supply in short time spent,
We hasten past what's truly ours,
And waste what jealousy devours.
The measure of our wants declare,
What jealousy and envy share,
Forever mired in want we feed,
Our taste for jealousy we need.

LOVE BUG

A pesky itch has overcome,
immunities I've had,
'gainst heart disease and even some,
infections now a fad.

It comes upon me in the night,
and under noonday sun.
Attacks I've had cause me some fright,
for sanity undone.

Heroic treatment must be bought!
A medical referral?
No need for diagnosis sought,
before I met that girl.

That itch has turned a running sore!
Internal putrefaction?
And yet my soul cries out for more!
Eternal satisfaction?

So what's the awful antidote?
Her casual caress?
Her serum's kiss my cheek be smote?
Her person I undress?

O, no! It's from the Love Bug's bite,
that I should suffer thus.
Prognosis dim! There's no respite!
And none to blame but us!

JOURNEY

My back-pack filled with secret dreams,
to crack the code of nature's schemes,
with confidence and hope devout,
upon an errant trek set out.

I saw old men with telescopes,
white coated labs and microscopes,
wild eyed, long haired misanthropes
and some who said they knew the ropes.

I even read some big, thick books,
and bought some tests from campus crooks,
walked columned halls, through lectures snored,
wore long black robe and mortar board.

But yet my dreams did not fulfill,
and nature's scheme a mystery still,
until a young girl's charm was lent,
a kiss her secret message sent.

LOVE'S PLIGHT

Oh would I could your name forget,
and from my mind at last erase,
your voice, your smile, your kiss, and yet,
I'll not forget your lovely face.

When last I pledged my heart to you,
as oft times had I sworn before,
there I among your suitors knew,
my oath of love you'd sure ignore.

Alone, adrift on sea of love,
of friendly ports are none in sight,
no one can know how hard I strove,
to get a date for Friday night.

TO WED

All those who walk the earth alone,
how lonely they must be,
to wake and find their years have flown,
their wholeness yet to see.

For so is nature's state of things,
when man his wife has won,
with solemn vows and trade of rings,
and two become as one.

It searched, my heart, the world around,
for one who held its key,
I thank my lucky stars it found,
the other half of me.

OUR TIME

If I could hold you in my arms again,
for just a little while,
what's left of all eternity....
's the least that I could ask.
If I could kiss you now,
just once before I die,
and feel your love upon my lips....
who knows how long a kiss may last?
The marvel of our time,
this time we call our own,
that piece of time since time began....
Just who, do you suppose,
arranged this time for us?

SHE'S HERE

In the quiet of the night she comes to me,
on a scent,
on a sound,
and somehow I know she speaks to me
on wisteria's breath in spring,
in autumn when cicadas sing,
in the creak of my old wooden chair
in the warmth of my fire
when wintry winds blow,
I know she's there.

Don't speak to me of lonliness,
cold rising from my bed.
I've put aside that terror now,
with all the tears I've shed.
It's comfort closing, closing me,
because I know she's here.

THE SUITOR

He called again at half past three,
and once again at four,
left notes of love writ pritily,
outside my chamber door.

O would his passion's season pass!
His ardor redirect!
toward other unsuspecting lass,
whose love's less circumspect.

While sweets and fragrant posies claim,
his love a prize today,
tomorrow brings another game,
with each new cards to play.

And hitherto the chaste he's chased,
surrendered 'twixt their sheets,
but I'll not see my chaste erased,
in love's gymnastics feats.

I'll take it as my role in life,
to bend him to my will,
content he'll be with me his wife,
his wand'ring eye be still.

MY HATE

With sun's first shining,
I enter my adopted state,
steely barred from reason,
and walled around with hate.

Clad in counterfeit grace,
my stoney heart concealed,
like brass overlayed with gold,
my true self is unrevealed.

To the Master's invitation,
followers at his table sup,
Deceipt and sham I brought,
with my hate filled cup.

Ease your hateful burden.
Take my bread and wine.
Give up yourself to love,
and declare yourself as mine.

No! Love is a hard master.
Brings only tears and pain.
My self to trade for that,
leaves naught for me to gain.

Bread and wine? Meager fare!
I crave a lustier plate.
I'll hold to all that's mine,
for I've learned to love my hate.

REMEMBER

Of all my fears in later years,
the fear I'd be forgot,
confounds my days with bitter tears,
and lonliness my lot.

The cure for dying all alone,
conceited minds agree,
I'll build a monument of stone,
and name it after me.

But stone is cold and mute to tell,
of all the loves I've lost,
of kisses shared in young love's spell,
while tender hearts were crossed.

What begs my mind's a schoolyard kiss,
a lifelong treasure be.
She'll not forget, that schoolyard Miss.
The boy she kissed was me.

FOR JOAN
On her sixtyfifth birthday...

What force aligns these orbs in space,
to each its path through heaven's void,
each star and planet in its place,
a plan that time has not alloyed.

And of man's kind am I alone?
Be none like me in places far?
Or just on this blue marble grown?
Beside this not top rated star?

And what's the force that guides my star?
that marks my birth, its reckoning,
and dictates what my fortunes are,
from pauper made perhaps a king?

Don't tell me chance all this controls!
Some long shot gamble's coin got tossed?
That made us one from two lost souls?
Sure not by lot our love not lost!

Dear Love, it's all one grand design!
What force but love all forces be,
The force that joins your life with mine!
The force that holds you close to me!

LORD

MORE

Oh why must I share God's blessings,
wasted on beasts lesser than I?
The tiger's content with stalking,
so what need has a bird to fly?

Take sounding whales, for example.
To surface they must by and by.
No hint of mystique about that.
The whale holds his breath same as I.

The working of bees we marvel,
but work of turtles is funny.
To compare that pair is unfair.
Bee's work is just making honey.

Cows give us milk. Hogs give us ham.
From beautiful trees we pick figs.
Consider this cunning program;
we don't waste our time milking pigs.

Cows give their milk while relaxing.
The pig's part's no effort at all.
God knows I've worked hard as a bee.
But my reward powers forestall.

All I have now is my beauty,
cash, coin and gemstones in store.
Only one thing left I yearn for;
Please let me have just a bit more.

FORGIVE

Just who amongst us dares not hide,
beneath his tougher, outer hide,
a rotted fruit when peeled aside,
reveals an ugly pit inside.

And count all those who have denied,
to honor truth; have sworn and lied,
and yet their innocence have cried,
when rule of law to them applied.

In book of life see names inscribed,
writ down for reason to be tried,
along with others who abide,
to let themselves fall prey to pride.

All these and more our faults we bear,
confined to human frame to live,
His promise is your burden share,
He will forgive, forgive, forgive.

KNOWLEDGE

With age comes lots
of aches and pains.
They come and go
like summer rains.

We'd never know
of pain they say
until we know
it's gone away.

We should give thanks
for feeling bad.
We'd not know glad
without some sad.

You gave to me
a valued friend,
How could I know
his days would end?

And so of love
and loss I've known.
With loss of love
my knowledge's grown.

That part of love
brings sorrow pains
like summer joy
in summer rains.

Then thank you, Lord,
for sorrow's pain,
and thank you, Lord
for summer's rain.

PRAYER

Dear Lord, how tender hangs the thread,
that parts the living from the dead.
Through hurts and harm, disease and years,
life clings to life on seas of tears.

But when her thread of life got frayed,
and now its break not be delayed,
then fall she will into Your han'
one life's ended, one new began.

Margaret, December 27, 2000

STARS

Why seek the wisdom of the stars,
flung out through space when God was young
when seed of man was yet unsown,
nor light nor life from earth was sprung.

From out His boundless mind He set
His eye upon eternity,
of time and space that knows no end,
its limit's He alone can see.

So now atop impertinence
you dare devine Him of His sphere,
Not so! Take comfort just to know,
God made it all and put it there.

Christmas, 2000

SPARK

How strange of all that God has made,
just one was blessed with human spark,
where love and grace and beauty stayed,
and yet possessed with light and dark.

In only one, for all we know,
beside just one bright glowing star,
the single place where life might grow,
'twas there that man invented war.

Since time began, from sire to son,
his killing engines got refined,
and legacy of death begun,
in ways to alter humankind.

Then more and more like beasts behave,
his blessings waste and evils flout,
and lives of future sons enslave---
Would God the human spark put out?

MY STARS

How eagerly the mountains rise,
to meet the setting sun,
his soft'ning rays at last apprise,
that evening's just begun.

From far beyond sun's fading hues,
a sparkling light appears,
a stellar herald's charge renews,
stars' vigils through the years.

And now bright starlight fills the night,
earth's endless cobalt dome,
each star a sun of unknown might,
perhaps an angel's home?

Stars near we know by name, but Oh!
what's on their other side?
The nest where future aeons grow?
where past tomorrows hide?

A moment now in space and time,
'tis mine by high decree,
my living license, proof that I'm
assured a place for me.

MIRACLE

Just who directs the Mockingbird
to pick the song he sings?
And who decides his song be heard
'mongst other songs in spring?

You hear the sound of geese in flight,
soft whispers from their wings,
declare the sum of nature's might,
the spectacle it brings.

Each dawn the sunrise bugle calls,
a miracle's at hand.
'Twixt birth and death a curtain falls,
you've yet to understand.

And still you're nature's child, you see,
like springtime's song, were born,
to rise and fly as birds, you're free,
before your curtain's torn.

PRAISE

And now as my lamp's flame burns low,
I search my brothers' mind's to know,
of all behind the veil they see,
for me remains a mystery.

From child size seats in Sunday School,
I learned that Grace of God would rule,
but wars and want are history's sum,
His promised kingdom's yet to come.

How oft' I've seen my brothers good,
in foreign places give their blood,
for petty passing man made cause,
or give reason man made laws.

And what say you of Golden Rule?
that practice makes a man a fool.
In love or trade no rule be fit,
he always wants the best of it.

My hopes for all mankind now fade,
for were we in His image made?
This sorry mold best be forgot,
but for the sake of Grace it's not.

And what of Grace do I deserve?
No less than others I observe.
Could now I hear my Master speak,
and tell me of the goal I seek.

Be still now my impatient one,
I gave to you my only Son.
Hate and greed are your invention.
Faith and love were my intention.

You grieve for blood and all mankind,
you must believe all that was mine.
I gave my Son that you may live,
and all your sins I would forgive.

It is eternal life I give,
and an enduring soul to live.
All this is yours for all your days.
Just raise your hands to me in praise.

A simple Christmas wish
December, 2000

DRINK DEEP

Drink deep the surging duskset breeze,
Its moon cooled fragrance borne,
And 'wake, man's ancient passions seize,
The night with reckless scorn.

And reckless seek the heat of night,
All senses tuned for her,
But senseless wrought by love's delight,
In lust that sense prefer.

Abandon now old lessons learned,
And yield to wanton flesh,
Like beasts afield base wants return,
Their instinct thirst refresh.

And now sun's light night's spell disperse,
To day's long work recall,
To suffer brightly day time's curse,
And wait for night to fall.

FLIGHT

Surrounded by the ones I love,
amid my keepsakes held so dear,
I've made my life a well worn glove,
absorbed in warmth and heart felt cheer.

All those who shared my youth are dead,
their day of life worn well past noon,
as oft' through time their perils fled,
amazed because 'twould end so soon.

And now my time's worn well past noon,
and oft' I've fled but not for fear,
my perils fell, amazed, too soon,
to see my race's end so near.

It's sunset now, my day has fled,
and soon will come my long sought night,
it's now I must prepare for bed,
amazed am I my beauteous flight.

SURPRISE

God's secret for tomorrow lies,
in trust for those who pray,
To know before of his surprise,
betrays His trust today.

Should fame and riches be your prize,
then pray for grace to share it,
Should pain and loss inspire your cries,
then pray for strength to bear it.

And when at last your last of days,
your final prize befall,
Your last of prayers be filled with praise,
His best surprise of all!

AFTERWORD

Afterword
by Steve Chase

When Dad entered his 70s my brothers and I asked him to write down some of his childhood memories and remembrances of the people he had encountered in his life--a kind of memoir. To ease the process, I gave him a dictation tape recorder and he proceeded to recite some hilarious, poignant stories from his youth. These may form the basis of another published work in the future.

A couple of years later he told me he was writing verse. This was not just your average poetry, mind you, this was really good, worthy-of-publishing-quality poetry, he said.

Those of us who have experienced his thought provoking wit know that his humor is often laced with outrageous, tongue-in-cheek comments. So my first thought was, "Right, Dad. Show me!"

When I received his first few poems, which he had typed on one of his antique typewriters, I had to admit that his muse had arrived--with bells on! This was some of the most insightful, beautifully constructed poetry I had ever read. But I'm just his kid, biases attached.

Ron Daniel, Dan Starkey and Luke's sons (Dave, Kirt and myself) have collected here most of the poems he has written in his 3 year poetry writing career. Hopefully his muse continues to inspire and there will be new verses for future collections.

Most of Luke's poems are written in one piece. The words come to him in a rush and he hurries to his computer (which has replaced the old typewriter) to get the poem down before the muse escapes. Some of them are sublime. Some evoke different meanings and messages upon re-reading. Some are just plain funny. All together they begin to reveal the depth of the rational and emotional sides of this remarkable man.

Feel free to email Luke with your impressions of this collection: LAbbottChase@aol.com
He would be delighted to hear from you.

Steve Chase
April 2003

Afterword 2

By David Chase

I have never been much of a fan of poetry. I'm not one to appreciate the illusory techniques or the poetic license that many poets can't resist. It seemed to me poets were like the beatniks of the fifties and sixties. Neurotic, self indulgent, counter culture, intellectual "wannabes". And yet, around three years ago, my father was inspired to begin writing verse.

My father, as you would expect, is the exception to my concept of a poet. He truly is an intellectual, with a voracious appetite for the written word. He prefers biographies, autobiographies and history. The American Civil War time period is almost an obsession. He has read every book written on the subject. In fact, many conversations find their way into a story from the Civil War.

Since my father's retirement from the Columbia Daily Tribune, he has been compelled to write critiques of the grammatical errors committed by the Tribune's staff writers. Incorrect usage of language drives him crazy, unless it is done for literary purpose. The 'Bune' has graciously printed some of his observations.

As I read my father's poetry, I get a glimpse of his inner thoughts and feelings. I feel like I've been on a journey through many facets of his life experience. I've enjoyed his intellectual observations, his unique sense of humor, his well hidden emotional side and his awe of the miracle that is the love and grace of our Lord.

Thank you God for inspiring my Dad to reveal himself.

David B. Chase
April, 2003

Afterword 3
By Kirt Chase

I was fortunate to be raised in a household that stressed the importance of language and how precious it is to our culture. All too often we are bombarded with slang and bad grammar from people in the media who should know better.

For as long as I can remember, my father has made good sport of pointing out these offenses, most glaring during the evening news. Is it too much to ask that someone on national television use proper grammar? As a kid I remember countless times my Dad explained that something a celebrity on television just said was grammatically incorrect!

How could this be? Those people on TV know everything! They have fancy clothes, lots of make-up and six figure salaries to prove it! But seriously, Dad was great at pointing out their many foibles and he taught me to question these "talking heads".

My father has always had a way with words. Good writing is like good music. It imparts thoughts and emotions to the beholder in a very special way. I think these poems have a way of finding a common denominator for many people. The reader can relate the feelings they invoke to similar experiences in their life.

It makes me very happy to see this book finished. Our family has enjoyed reading my father's poetry for the last few years. Like loose photographs they deserve to be in a complete collection.

Copies of this book are being donated to school and public libraries throughout the state of Missouri. I am proud to know that scores of people will enjoy these works for years to come. I have always admired those who can create something so lasting and permanent that they achieve a kind of immortality. This book is just such a creation. It will stand forever as a record of a life well lived.

Kirt Chase
April, 2003

TRIBUTES

His Mark's On Me

———————

Walking through the door that day
I really didn't have a clue,
Asking to talk to "Mr. Chase"
was something, as a lark, I chose to do.

He approached the front counter
and asked what, for me, he could do?
I said, "Give me a chance to hire on here
and go to work for you."

Looking at me intently,
He asked if I had a journalism degree?
I told him "No, I had a wife, new child
and a discharge from the Navy."

"Well then," he exclaimed, "With no
training or background, my question becomes why?"
I said, "Does Mike Brooks work for you?
If he can do it, so can I."

With that saucy quip, I enticed a laugh
and he said "I like your style"
"There may be changes coming so
keep in touch," and he followed with a smile.

Well, I kept in touch and true to word
Luke gave me a chance one day.
Showed me what a pica was, where the mats were
and then sent me on my way.

To cruise up and down Broadway
peddling advertising wares.
Come back, write copy, do layouts
and then send everything upstairs.

Ahh, upstairs to composing where we
hoped they would accommodate
We couldn't touch anything up there
or cracked knuckles were our fate

Glen Ogle Hill was the unions'
enforcer whose prosthesis was really bad
He'd weave and wobble over to you
and you knew your hand was had

This was my start
in a career unforeseen
From advertising to composing
and back somewhere in between

Luke taught me well and gave me
more than I can repay
Phrases like, "Boone County French,"
"Scotch whipsky" and "dig es vous?" to say

A love of classical music from
1812 Overture to Pathetiqué;
And an appreciation of good scotch
along with raw meat to eat

But more than that he nurtured and
gave me a chance to shine
To work with others unselfishly
and develop untapped skills of mine.

All those things and more have worked
to shape my very life,
Even how to conduct myself going
from my first to second wife.

People who have profound impact on your life
can be counted on one hand you see.
There are only two, other than my wife and mother,
And their initials are L and JC.

Ron Daniel
March 2003

P.S. Thank you Luke for your gift of counsel, caring and friendship. You influenced us more than you'll ever know. With this book, we give you our love and homage.

Abbott!

In my life there have been four people other than my father who have had a hand in shaping my career.

My first boss, Jack Nowell of Nowell's Grocery, Henry J. Waters iii, editor and publisher of The Columbia Tribune, Robert M. White ii editor and publisher of The Mexico Ledger and Luke Abbott Chase.

Mr. Chase or ABBOTT as he was affectionately known by his minions was the ad director of the Tribune. He was more than just a boss. He was a teacher, a mentor, and neighbor and a friend.

He took a group of wild and crazy young men and women and molded them into a dominant ad sales force that even Hank Waters would grudgingly admit was one of the most productive sales teams ever to sell for the Tribune.

Luke managed, or maybe a better term would be corralled, the likes of Vernie, Rollo,

Starkblum, Cheeks, Skaggman Don, Doberman Dee, the Gray Fox and Joe Mama. A rag tag group of long haired but mostly bright-eyed kids that refused to fail.

Some were excellent salespeople.

Some were excellent graphic designers.

Some were artists.

Some, believe it or not had the patience for detail. (I'd rather call it an affliction).

All of us had one thing in common. We wanted to be winners. We wanted to be successful. Not just for ourselves but for Luke. We didn't want to disappoint him and all of us worked as a team to keep that from happening.

It was the early '70s. Luke was a hypersensitive, nervous skinny man and our staff caused most of his problems. I can remember times in the old Tribune when we would have a quick sales meeting in the upstairs breakroom. Luke was so nervous he couldn't drink a cup of coffee without spilling it and our group delighted in his predicament.

Luke tried hard to manage this group but at best he just guided us. He would do all the things a manager should do. He would set a sales goal for a special section and build graphs for the wall. The deadline would be friday at 5 p.m. for 2000 inches. At 3 p.m. our staff may have logged 500 inches as a group. We purposely held back posting our sold ads until the absolute deadline to drive Luke crazy.

Time erases some of the memory but I believe we exceeded most of those goals and succeeded in giving Luke a few more gray hairs in his crew cut. That was certainly our goal.

All good things end. Eventually the group wanted to try their hand at other ventures. We started as kids working hard and playing harder. We left the Tribune as advertising professionals to pursue our dreams.

Today, a couple of those kids are running their own marketing companies. Two more are publishing daily newspapers. One is the head of a book/magazine printing company and a couple of others left the business to get real jobs.

Luke's " kids" turned out to be quasi professional successful adults and I believe if you asked any one of them they would tell you "ABBOTT" played an important part in their maturation process. He taught us how to negotiate with difficult people. He taught us tolerance. He taught us the value of teamwork. He taught us to appreciate good Scotch whisky and eat raw meat. He helped us manage money and buy houses.........

But most of all He taught us to believe in ourselves and encouraged us to pursue our dreams.

For this and a hundred other reasons I am eternally greatful. Long live L. Abbott.

Joe A. May
"Joe Mama"
Publisher
Mexico Ledger
Mexico Mo.

All the bad things...

So you're expecting another tribute to Luke
Chase. Yeah, right! I suppose he deserves an
accolade or two. But it's always been much eas-
ier for me to point out the obvious flaws in one's
personage. It's not something of which I am
necessarily proud, it's just the way it is. Besides,
knowing everyone else would take the high
road and be overly complimentary, I figured I
would take just a few minutes and list all the
bad things that can be said about Luke Chase.

However, I must say it was Luke that finally gave
me the chance to realize my dream of working
for the Columbia Daily Tribune. I say finally,
because I was rejected on many previous
attempts. The first was when I lost my bid to
become a Tribune carrier to Larry Joe Stark. But
hey, he had a bicycle and even then I under-
stood the importance of getting the news deliv-
ered in a timely manner.

My first introduction to L. Abbott Chase came a
few years later while I was still in high school.
I ventured into the 'Bune one day looking for

part time work. I remember talking to Chase, Francis Pike, Alan Leach, Gordon Zimmerman, and anyone else with any hiring authority that would take the time to tell me "Sorry, we just don't have anything you could do." Rejection, as they say, is just part of the process.

Anyway, a few weeks later I returned to the 'Bune as part of my duties as business manager of the high school newspaper. As I was talking to Alan Leach, a whistling Chase skipped by and stopped abruptly (probably thought I was begging for work again) and asked, "Do you still want to work here." I said, "You bet." Chase explained he needed somebody to run proofs. Thus, I began my all too brief association with Luke and the Tribune by being the best darned proof runner they ever had. (I didn't say the best looking, just the best).

As time passed Luke assigned me a few accounts and it was with his patient direction and tutelage that he developed my layout skills to the level required to take over the always-challenging Temple Stephens ad.

Unfortunately, I had to take some time out of my stint with the 'Bune to tour Vietnam. When I returned, Luke was one of the first people I called. (I really was begging for work this time). Sadly, he informed me he didn't need anybody at the time, but stay in touch. Timing, as they say is everything. And so, whether out of pity or necessity, Luke called a few weeks later and said he had a spot for me. The timing was perfect for me since I was about out of beer money.

Over the next couple of years Luke provided the guidance that helped me grow from a kid that didn't know shit into a young man that didn't know shit. But hey, we had a lot of fun. There have been many times I wish I would have hung around longer.

Anyway back to my list. The minutes have now turned into hours. This is taking much longer than I thought it would. I know it would be a whole lot easier if I were standing next to the fidgety old fart. Lord knows there's plenty of material to work with.

I do think that whole Don Knotts "nervous guy"

routine was just an act anyway. With the young, enthusiastic and talented staff Luke assembled to provide the bulk of revenue required to keep the Tribune in business – what did he have to be nervous about anyway. Besides, whenever he wanted to have a sales meeting, all he had to do was go up to Harpo's.

One of Luke's greatest strengths was to lead by example. I especially remember the time when Luke instituted the "cursing can" in response to many complaints from other departments about the ad sales team's less than businesslike language. Anytime someone used foul language they had to donate some change to the can. For a while, this innovation proved to be less than successful. Then one day, Luke stomped in, with arms flailing, cursing up a storm and continued to swear incessantly as he threw money at the can with both hands. I think it was then that we all realized just how unprofessional our actions had been.

But seriously, Luke does deserve the credit for putting together the greatest newspaper ad sales team ever - and having enough sense to stay out of the way. Thanks, Luke, for allowing me to be a part of it and sharing some of the best times I've ever had. The team Luke put together was one that blended incredibly well and really fed off each other's talents. Part of the synergy that developed was because we helped each other to grow and delighted in each other's success...and made each other better. For instance, I know it was no coincidence that my ad layouts started looking a whole lot better when Joe May joined the staff.

Anyway, back to my list. The hours have now turned into days. I will say I enjoyed mentally rehashing what I remember about Luke and the team. I laughed a whole lot and even cried a little. Thanks, guys, for allowing me to do that. But finally, I finished my list. Following are all the bad things that can be said about Luke Chase:

Jerry Bledsoe
"Geraldine DeBedsore"
April 2003